The Rocky Mountain States

T0002327

Jennifer Prior, Ph.D.

Consultant
Brian Allman
Principal
Upshur County Schools, West Virginia

Publishing Credits
Rachelle Cracchiolo, M.S.Ed., *Publisher*
Emily R. Smith, M.A.Ed., *SVP of Content Development*
Véronique Bos, *VP of Creative*
Dona Herweck Rice, *Senior Content Manager*
Dani Neiley, *Editor*
Fabiola Sepulveda, *Series Graphic Designer*

Image Credits: p9 Wikimedia Commons; p10 Boston Public Library Tichnor Brothers collection; p11 (top) Alamy Stock Photo/Robert E. Barber; p11 (middle) Shutterstock/Teresa Otto; p12–13 Alamy Stock Photo/directphoto.bz; p13 (top) Thierry Berrod, Mona Lisa Productions/Science Source; p13 (bottom) Herb Bryce; p14 Alamy Stock Photo/WorldPhotos; p15 (top) Alamy Stock Photo/Classic Image; p16 (bottom) Library of Congress [LC-DIG-ppmsca-09855]; p17 Getty Images/DEA Picture Library; p18 Newscom/Luc Novovitch DanitaDelimont.com/Danita Delimont Photography; p20 Getty Images/MediaNews Group/Boulder Daily Camera; p21 Getty Images/Lyn Alweis; p22 Associated Press; p23 (top) Alamy Stock Photo/Science History Images; p23 (bottom) Charles Roscoe (Savage, C. R.); p25 Alamy Stock Photo/The Bookworm Collection; p25 (bottom) Getty Images/Bloomberg; all other images from iStock and/or Shutterstock

Library of Congress Cataloging-in-Publication Data
Names: Prior, Jennifer Overend, 1963- author.
Title: The Rocky Mountain states / Jennifer Prior.
Description: Huntington Beach, CA : Teacher Created Materials, [2022] |
    Includes index. | Audience: Grades 4-6 | Summary: "The Rocky Mountain
    states-miles and miles of untouched land and not a person in sight.
    While that may be true in some places, these states are also quite
    populated and modern. They are rich in history and steeped in American
    Indian culture. Running through all these states are the majestic Rocky
    Mountains. People come from all over to enjoy outdoor activities and
    amazing sights"-- Provided by publisher.
Identifiers: LCCN 2022021235 (print) | LCCN 2022021236 (ebook) | ISBN
    9781087691039 (paperback) | ISBN 9781087691190 (ebook)
Subjects: LCSH: Rocky Mountains Region--Juvenile literature. | West
    (U.S.)--Juvenile literature.
Classification: LCC F721 .P75 2022 (print) | LCC F721 (ebook) | DDC
    978--dc23/eng/20220502
LC record available at https://lccn.loc.gov/2022021235
LC ebook record available at https://lccn.loc.gov/2022021236

**Shown on the cover is Longs Peak above Bear
Lake in Rocky Mountain National Park.**

This book may not be reproduced or distributed in any
way without prior written consent from the publisher.

5482 Argosy Avenue
Huntington Beach, CA 92649
www.tcmpub.com
ISBN 978-1-0876-9103-9
© 2023 Teacher Created Materials, Inc.

Table of Contents

caribou in the Rocky
Mountain foothills

Today's Rocky Mountain Region

When you think of the Rocky Mountain region, you may think of miles of wilderness without a person in sight. While that is somewhat true, today's Rocky Mountain states are quite different. This region includes the states of Colorado, Idaho, Montana, Utah, Wyoming, and New Mexico.

The Rocky Mountain region is diverse. It consists of small towns, big cities, and large expanses of **scenic** wonder. It is rich in history and steeped in American Indian culture. Running through it all are the majestic Rocky Mountains.

This huge mountain range brings tourism to these states. People visit to see wildlife. They come for outdoor sports, camping, and fishing. Cities in this area are bustling and modern. Local shops and museums are found in each one.

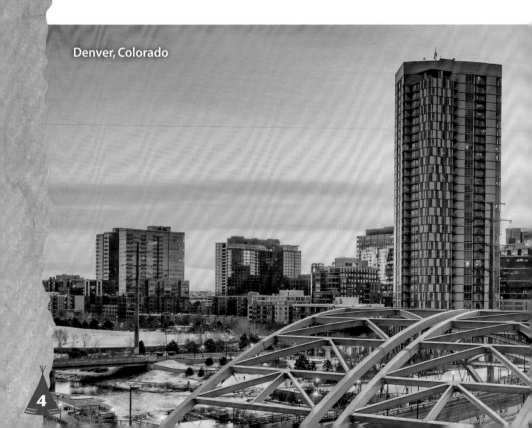

Denver, Colorado

Old West Town

How did Steamboat Springs, Colorado, get its name? A nearby spring shot water out of the ground. When it did, it made a chugging sound like a steamboat. Legend has it that a trapper heard the noise and said, "There's a steamboat, by gar!"

Some parts of the region are, indeed, wild even today. A hiker using a GPS watch to **navigate** a trail might encounter a bobcat or a bear. And that same hiker might be able to find cell reception to call home to tell them all about it. It's a mix of the old, the new, and the wilderness of an amazing mountain range. This is where the Rocky Mountains meet the modern age!

Georgetown,
Colorado, 1859

The Rocky Mountain States

The West makes up almost half of the United States. Some of these states are **coastal**. They have borders that rest along the Pacific Ocean. Some of the states are part of the Southwest. These have large expanses of desert. They are heavily influenced by Mexican culture. And five of the western states are nestled into the world's second-longest mountain range—the Rocky Mountains.

Western Hot Spot

Rocky Mountain National Park is a popular spot for tourists. The park is visited by more than three million people every year. It has 124 named peaks, many of which reach up to the alpine tundra. This is the part of mountains that is up so high that trees cannot grow there.

San Juan Mountains, Colorado

The Rocky Mountains are also known as the Rockies. While the states in this region have cultures and **terrains** all their own, they share many similarities. The Rocky Mountain states have wide-open spaces. They have mild, dry summers. Snow falls in most places during the winter months. They attract tourism for skiing and other outdoor sports. And the mountains that pass through each of these states look and feel enormous. Traveling through these mountains used to be a difficult task. But modern roads now make these wilderness areas easy to access. In fact, millions of people visit these states each year to experience their **solitude** and wonder.

The Rocky Mountains begin in northern Canada. They end in northern New Mexico. They span 3,000 miles (4,800 kilometers)! In some places, the mountain range is 300 miles (482 kilometers) wide. That's almost as wide as the state of Arizona. The highest peak is Mount Elbert in Colorado. It is 14,440 feet (4,401 meters) high.

The Rockies are home to many animals. Black bears, grizzly bears, mountain lions, and bighorn sheep live there. In addition to these large mammals, many birds, snakes, rodents, and river otters call this area home.

Rugged, Rocky Mountain Lady

The rugged Rockies might seem like a difficult place to live. But Isabella Bird did not shy away from them. She was a travel writer who lived in the Rockies in the late 1880s. She even climbed a mountain that was 14,259 feet (4,346 meters) high wearing a silk dress!

Rocky Mountain National Park is in Colorado. It is a popular tourist destination with a lot to do and see. Trail Ridge Road is a paved road in the park. It is called the Highway to the Sky for good reason. Imagine a winding road heading toward a vast, blue sky. Along the way are places to stop and see amazing views. And one of the most popular sights to see? That's the Continental Divide.

The Continental Divide is a natural boundary. It divides North America's river systems. Water from snow and rain that falls on the west side of the divide flows to the Pacific Ocean. When it falls on the east side of the divide, it flows to the Atlantic Ocean.

While several states share the Rockies, each has its own unique sights. The Rocky Mountain states are full of natural landmarks. There are unique bodies of water and stunning rock formations. Here are just a few of the most well-known sights:

The Silent City of Rocks is in Idaho. This landmark has more than 5,000 feet (1,524 meters) of **exposed** granite. Granite is a very hard rock. Many years of exposure to weather have eroded the softer rock around it. Interesting rock shapes and tall **spires** were left behind.

City of Rocks National Reserve, Idaho

Prehistoric Turtle

The Hell Creek Formation has a fossil of a triceratops! The fossils there go from huge to very small. Here is a fossil of a turtle called a Trionyx.

Montana is home to the Hell Creek Formation. It is made of sandstone, shale, and a type of coal called lignite. The formation contains fossils of dinosaurs, primates, and many small animals. It is believed that an asteroid hit this area at some point. It left behind a metal called **iridium**.

Is it possible to stand in the water of two oceans at the same time? Well, in Wyoming it is! Two Oceans Creek splits into the Atlantic Creek and the Pacific Creek. The water from one creek goes to the Atlantic Ocean, and the other heads off to the Pacific.

Carter County Museum, Montana

Hell Creek Formation, Montana

11

Bryce Canyon is in southern Utah. It has many unique rock formations. Irregular columns of rock are called *hoodoos*. Bryce Canyon has more hoodoos than any other place on the planet. Years of erosion from wind and water have resulted in sandstone formations like nowhere else. Two very popular sites at Bryce Canyon are Wall Street and the Alligator. The Wall Street rocks are high columns that look like tall buildings. The Alligator is not a hoodoo yet. It has not finished forming. You can see the rock that has not yet eroded away into columns. At the top in the center, it looks like a giant rock alligator is stretched out in the sun.

the Alligator at Bryce Canyon

Colorado has many natural landmarks. One that is very interesting (and stinky) is Sulphur Cave. This landmark is in the northwestern part of the state. The air inside the cave is toxic from sulfur. People who explore there have to wear gas masks. Surprisingly enough, there are creatures that survive and **thrive** in Sulphur Cave, such as bloodworms and bacteria. You may know of **stalactites** that hang inside caves. Well, Sulphur Cave has snottites that look like — you guessed it—drips of snot!

snottites

Ebenezer's Canyon

Bryce Canyon was named after a Mormon pioneer. His name was Ebenezer Bryce. He and his family settled there in 1875. He built an irrigation ditch and a road. These helped the nearby town of Clifton.

History of the Rocky Mountain States

For centuries, American Indian tribes lived in the Rockies. This was a place rich in food to gather and hunt. Nations such as the Nimiipuu, Dakota, Shoshone, and Ute lived there. They spent the fall and winter hunting bison on the plains. In the spring and summer, they moved into the mountains to hunt deer and elk. They also caught fish and gathered berries.

The Dakota people had a deep connection to the land. Everyone in their community had a role. Women were the "keepers of the home." They farmed, weaved clothes, and gathered wood. In the spring, the Dakota people moved to sugaring camps where they made maple syrup.

The Shoshone people were also skilled hunters and gatherers. They moved with the seasons, migrating to find resources when the weather changed. In October, they gathered pinyon nuts, a key part of their diet in the winter months.

Dakota women preparing dinner

Ute Chief Sevara and his family, 1899

The Ute people took care of the land they lived on. When it came to wild plants, they gathered only what they needed to survive. They hunted and gathered in different places throughout the year so the land could restore itself.

Signs of the tribes who lived in the Rockies long ago still exist. To keep wild game in their territory, some tribes built walls along the top of the Continental Divide. Some of the walls are still there.

The Nimiipuu Peoples

The Nimiipuu people were also nomadic hunters. In the 18th century, they began hunting with horses. The Nimiipuu people soon had one of the largest horse herds. They are known for creating the Appaloosa horse breed.

Lewis and Clark

In the early 1800s, a team of men set off on a journey. One of their leaders was Meriwether Lewis. The other was William Clark. They set forth to see parts of the United States that had never been explored by Europeans. The journey ultimately took them through what are now the states of Montana and Idaho. Tribes had already lived in this area for many years.

Westward Expansion

President Thomas Jefferson liked the idea of expanding west. He believed it was the best way for the nation to grow. He bought a large piece of land that included the Rocky Mountains. This was called the Louisiana Purchase. By the mid-1800s, thousands of American settlers began to travel across the wild terrain. They set up new homes there. They hoped for better lives.

American Progress by John Gast, 1872

Sand Creek Massacre

Conflicts with Tribes

Life was mostly peaceful for the tribes until these settlers began to move west. The tribes were forced to stay on land called **reservations**. This devastated their ability to hunt. They could no longer follow bison, a major source of food. Members of some tribes, such as the Cheyenne peoples, tried to remain peaceful. They did not want to fight back. But in 1864, the Sand Creek Massacre took the lives of more than 230 Cheyenne when **militiamen** attacked them in Colorado. Upon hearing this, the people of other tribes began to fight back.

Crazy Horse Memorial, South Dakota

Crazy Horse

Crazy Horse was the leader of the Lakota tribe. When he was young, he had a vision about how to dress and prepare for battle. He fought many times against settlers that moved into tribal territory.

American Indian Tribes Then and Now

American Indian tribes in the West suffered losses of land and freedom. Westward expansion caused many lives to be lost. Life for American Indian tribes now is very different compared to the past.

Some of these tribes still live in the Rocky Mountains today. Some choose to live on reservations. Others live in towns and cities. They carry on their tribal **traditions**.

Two tribes in Idaho decided to live as one. They are the Shoshone-Bannock tribe. They now live in southeastern Idaho. Their traditional way of life included hunting and gathering. The tribe continues to hunt and fish. Songs and stories are shared during these activities. This helps keep the tribes' cultural identity alive. Every August, there is the Shoshone-Bannock Indian Festival. Dancers and drum groups come together. It is a large cultural celebration.

Shoshone-Bannock Festival

Representing Her Tribe

Taylor Haskett is a member of the Shoshone-Bannock tribe. She works at a school. But she also competes in pageants. In 2017, it was the Miss Indian World contest. For the contest, she had to show a talent. She performed tribal storytelling.

The Blackfeet Nation is in northwest Montana. The tribe's name comes from the color of their shoes, which they paint with ashes. The tribe has over one million acres of land along the east side of the Rockies. Almost half of the tribe's members live on or near the tribal land. The tribe runs many businesses. Farming and ranching are the main industries. Farmers grow wheat, barley, and hay.

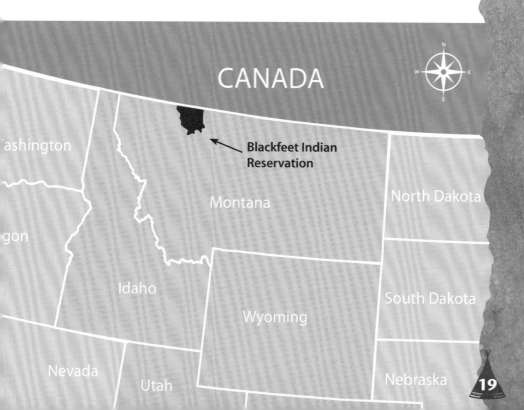

Blackfeet Indian Reservation

The Wind River Indian Reservation is in Wyoming. It is home to the Northern Arapaho and Eastern Shoshone tribes. The tribes share their history and culture with visitors. In the summer, different tribes host powwows. These are celebrations where people dance and gather with friends. It is also a way for tribes to honor their past. Visitors are welcome to share in the celebrations.

Utah has several small reservations. Some extend into other states. The Navajo Nation is in southeast Utah as well as Arizona, New Mexico, and Colorado. It is the largest tribe in the United States. The Navajo peoples have deep-rooted traditions. They also value humor. When a Navajo baby laughs for the first time, there is a laughing ceremony. The person behind the baby's giggle hosts a large feast to celebrate. The ceremony welcomes the baby into the community.

Arapaho tribe members

The Southern Ute tribe is in Colorado. They have events throughout the year that celebrate their culture. The Bear Dance is held in the spring. The dance tells the story of two brothers who went hunting. One of the brothers met a bear. The bear taught him a dance and a song to go with it. The Bear Dance event is open to the public. The tribe also has a spiritual ceremony. It is called the Sun Dance. This is their most important event of the year.

A Ute language teacher helps students at a Ute Reservation school.

Hide Painting

Painting animal hide is an art form for the Eastern Shoshone. This painting on an elk hide shows the Sun Dance. The artist used natural pigments to make the different colors.

Civic Engagement

We can all make a difference in the places we live. And one thing is true of the Rocky Mountain region: people care about their states. They encourage everyone to get involved.

People in Montana created a campaign called Public Lands in Public Hands. Its focus is on the Montana outdoor way of life. It works to protect public land.

4-H volunteer

Idaho's 4-H Youth Development programs help young people make a difference. Some teens work to expand 4-H programs. Others learn to use their creativity to express themselves. These programs encourage teens to be leaders in the state.

The Malcolm Wallop Civic Engagement program is in Wyoming. This group works with colleges. They get people talking. The focus is on conversations about key issues in the state.

Helping Others

The state of Utah has a large number of citizens who volunteer. In fact, it ranked number one in the United States. A study done by the organization Volunteering in America determined this in 2019. They found that 51 percent of people in Utah volunteer.

bioblitz at Glacier National Park, Montana

Throughout the Rocky Mountain region, an important concern is the environment. One way the community cares for the environment is through a bioblitz. In a bioblitz, experts come together to identify as many species in an area as they can. They work together in a short amount of time to name those species so that they can be studied and protected.

The Women's Foundation of Colorado helps women reach their goals. The group supports women and families. They work for positive change.

Utah also offers strong support for women. It was one of the first states to allow women to vote. Utah also had the first female senator. A 2016 study showed that women in Utah care deeply about many social issues. They want quality education and health programs. They help those who are experiencing homelessness.

Martha Hughes Cannon, Utah's first female senator

The Rocky Mountain States' Economy

The wide-open spaces of the West make perfect spots for food production. Open space means land for cattle. It means land for farming. And while this is true for all five of the Rocky Mountain states, their economies are made up of so much more.

Idaho is known for the making of computers, electronics, and medical equipment.

Montana is a big tourist spot. The state earns money from visitors to national parks. Millions come to visit each year. The state provides energy resources, such as coal and oil. It also makes electric power from wind and moving water.

While farming is one of its main industries, Wyoming makes most of its money from under the ground. Coal, natural gas, and crude oil are used for fuel and are just a few of its hidden treasures.

Colorado also has farming and mining. But this state is known for advanced technology as well.

Utah has stunning rock formations on the ground, but its main industry is "out of this world." It is one of the top states for making materials and vehicles for space travel.

cattle ranch in Colorado

Dry Farming

In the 1800s, many people in Wyoming began dry farming. This is a method of farming that uses only water from rainfall. Farmers check the soil often. They try different ways to keep it moist.

wind farm in Utah

spacecraft parts manufacturing in Utah

Salt Lake City, Utah

Tamed and Untamed

Some people think of the Rocky Mountain region as wild and untamed. And it is true that much of nature is still untouched there. But the region also has a modern edge. Big cities, such as Denver, are dotted across the states. Each one is home to people from a variety of backgrounds. These cities are also filled with thriving businesses.

The Rocky Mountain states are beautiful and unique. Tourists are drawn to them for their vast open spaces. Red rock formations and grand mountain ranges amaze those who visit. People are drawn to live there for the diverse lifestyle. They enjoy a strong economy. American Indian communities continue their tribal traditions. They often invite the public to share in and learn about their cultures.

The Rocky Mountain area is a thriving economic region. It provides the nation with food, fuel, and some of the most high-tech ideas. The states encourage their citizens to get involved and make a difference. The Rocky Mountain region is a land like no other and is filled with beauty and wonder.

Bison Return

Bison were almost hunted to extinction in the Old West. By 1889, there were fewer than one thousand left. Now, Yellowstone National Park is home to the largest herd of free-range bison. More than five thousand of them live there.

Map It!

Choose one of the Rocky Mountain states (Colorado, Idaho, Montana, Utah, or Wyoming) and make an "old" map of it. This is a map that future generations might find to see what the "old days" (today!) were like. Here is what you will do:

1. Research online to find major cities for your state. Locate the Rocky Mountains and national parks. Identify the American Indian reservations. Also find major lakes, rivers, and natural landmarks.
2. Cut out one large side of a big paper bag. Tear along the edges to make it look rough. Then, lay it flat with the printed side facedown.
3. Use permanent markers to draw the outline of the state and the features you found in your research. Use different colors, but be sure to use permanent markers.
4. Add a compass rose to show north, south, east, and west.
5. Now, age your map. Crumple it up and open it back up. Crumple it up again. Do this several times to make the map look old. The paper should also feel softer as the fibers break down. You can even soak it in water for a few minutes and then lay it out to dry.
6. Display your completed map, and tell your classmates about it, drawing attention to all the unique features of the state.

Boise, Idaho

Shoshone Falls, Twin Falls, Idaho

29

Glossary

coastal—bordering the ocean

exposed—not shielded or protected from weather

iridium—a metal that resists corrosion

militiamen—men who serve as soldiers in emergencies

navigate—to travel on, over, or through a place

reservations—areas of land set aside for American Indian tribes

scenic—having beautiful, natural scenery and views

solitude—the state of being alone

spires—tall, pointed objects

stalactites—icicle-like mineral formations found in caves

terrains—areas of land that share certain features

thrive—to develop very well

traditions—customs and beliefs that are passed down in families or other groups of people

Glacier National Park, Montana

Index

Learn More!

Sacagawea was a great help to Meriwether Lewis and William Clark as they explored the West. She spoke two American Indian languages. She taught Lewis and Clark survival skills. Because she was from the land that is now Idaho, she knew the region well.

✳ Research to learn more about this amazing woman.

✳ Use the facts you find to make a poster or mini book about her.

Sacagawea communicating with the native peoples